IMAGES
of America

WILLOWS

The Willows Depot, Crawford Hotel, and Hochheimer's store are at the intersection of Sycamore and Tehama Streets, seen here before that road was paved. Note the "Land and Water" for sale sign on the eaves of the Crawford. The town was growing rapidly. (Courtesy of the Museum Society of Willows.)

ON THE COVER: Farm workers are shown enjoying a refreshing treat of ripe, freshly picked watermelon, especially fine on a hot summer day. (Courtesy of the Museum Society of Willows.)

IMAGES
of America

WILLOWS

Museum Society of Willows,
J. Wright, and E. Whisman

ARCADIA
PUBLISHING

Published by Arcadia Publishing
Charleston, South Carolina

Library of Congress Control Number: 2009942101

For all general information contact Arcadia Publishing at:
Telephone 843-853-2070
Fax 843-853-0044
E-mail sales@arcadiapublishing.com
For customer service and orders:
Toll-Free 1-888-313-2665

Visit us on the Internet at www.arcadiapublishing.com

The Weinrich children, Leo, Bill, Frances, and George, are shown in 1904 with their goat and wagon as their proud mother looks on.

CONTENTS

DEDICATION

FRANCES LAUREL KING
MAY 26, 1911–JANUARY 20, 2004

Frances Laurel King was a longtime friend of the Willows Museum. She served on the board of directors and as a docent for many years. She had a wealth of knowledge relative to local history and eagerly shared her stories. In addition, she financially supported the museum in many small ways during her life and upon her death became a major benefactor.

Frances was a lifelong Willows resident, attending Willows schools and graduating from Glenn County High School. She received a bachelor of arts degree from Chico Normal School in 1932. She had two major careers: teaching and owning and operating the Land Title Company. She taught school in many grades and subjects until her retirement in 1966, when she was recognized for her outstanding teaching abilities and influence upon young people. In 1982, she was inducted into the Glenn County Educators Hall of Fame. Like her older sister, Jessie, and her twin sister, Alice, Frances was considered a civic leader, one who truly loved and gave generously to her community.

Because of Frances King's generosity to the Willows Museum, long-needed repairs were accomplished, displays were refurbished, and a general upgrading of artifact care and storage has been initiated, all under the motivation and implementation of a newly appointed board of directors. In addition, as the interesting photograph collection was revealed, this picture book came into being. It is altogether fitting that this book is dedicated to Frances Laurel King.

Frances Laurel King
May 26, 1911–January 20, 2004

ACKNOWLEDGMENTS

Photographs used in the Willows book are the property of the Museum Society of Willows, with the exception of those loaned by Baird Weinrich. We especially thank Donna Chittenden for her time and expertise with photographs and Ed Schnurbusch for his contribution of historic pictures.

Information sources have included Joan Bartalini, Bob Chittenden, Bill and Nettie Flanagan, Ed Schnurbusch, Jim and Velma Spurlock, and Baird Weinrich.

Support and assistance was given by Clifta Atlas, JoAnne Bond, Dr. Bill Wesley Brown, Ray Crabtree, Joan Cronk, Carolyn Davis, Oliver Hill, Curtis Hurlburt, Barbara Mann, Shirley Pattison, Vickie Torrey, Peter Towne, Byron Whisman, Carlton Wright, and the Wal-Mart Photography Department.

Posthumous recognition is given to the following for their preservation of historic photographs and information: Ethel Baker, Elizabeth Eubank, Charles "Smokey" Henry, and Bill Weinrich. Thank you ALL!

INTRODUCTION

In the early days, the land on which Willows now stands was known as the plains. It was covered with succulent native grasses. Will S. Green wrote, "Along the paths made by the Indians, I wandered back toward the plains. . . as beautiful a scene as ever met the vision of man. There was one endless sea of white and blue, purple and gold. It seemed a sea, as the gentle breeze made these myriads of wild flowers wave and glisten in the sun. I seemed to be reveling in a very Garden of Eden, and I wondered if God had made for Adam a more beautiful paradise."

There was a spring-fed pond east of the present town site. It was a memorable landmark on the treeless plains as it was surrounded by willow trees and could be seen from miles around, hence the name of "the Willows." It provided water for range cattle, and it is said that the Wintun Indians lived there long before white men began exploring Northern California.

The first settlers of what was then the northern part of Colusa County took up land along the Sacramento River and waterways coming from the Coast Range Mountains to the west. By the early 1870s, newcomers began to locate on the plains near the Willows. Farming was becoming extensive in the area, and land could be bought for $4–$6 an acre. One such newcomer was Daniel Zumwalt.

In 1876, Zumwalt struck a deal with railroad magnate Charlie Crocker, whose Northern Railway Company was wending its way up the west side of the Sacramento Valley. In exchange for a portion of Zumwalt's land, the railroad company would have its right-of-way, railroad surveyors would map out a 34-block town, and Zumwalt would receive half of the proceeds for each town lot sold. These lots sold rapidly, and by the end of 1876, there were three hotels, two livery stables, two saddlery and harness shops, one grocery store, one liquor store, one butcher shop, two saloons, three blacksmith shops, one boot and shoe store, one photography salon, and one doctor. There were just under 500 people living in this bustling community, and when the first train arrived on September 26, 1878, a great celebration took place, complete with a brass band.

As the town continued its commercial and industrial growth, its spiritual, educational, and social needs were also fulfilled as the town came together.

Between 1873 and 1893, five churches were established in Willows. They were the Baptist church, Methodist church, Catholic church, Christian church, and Episcopal church.

The first school was built in 1878 where the present-day memorial hall stands. Within 12 years it was outgrown, and the Willows Grammar School was erected in its place. This one was replaced in 1922 by the Sycamore Elementary School, and in 1975, it was replaced by the Willows Intermediate School. Before the first high school was built in 1903, high school students attended classes on the second floor of the grammar school. When the 1903 high school was outgrown, a new facility was built in 1918. This school burned in 1942 and was not replaced until 1949, and in the meantime, students attended classes in old houses moved into the vicinity.

Before the town ever began, a Jockey Club was organized by the settlers on July 5, 1876. J. R. Troxel was elected president and W. H. Kelley elected secretary. In May 1886, the club became the Willows Agricultural Association and acquired 60-plus acres in east Willows (an area later known as the Pittsburg Addition). It was east of the railroad tracks between present-day State Highway 162 and Glenn County Road 51. It had a fence surrounding it, with a grandstand on what is now Yolo Street. Horse racing was one of the largest social events of the year, and it took place in August and lasted one week.

Music was an important part of the settlers' social life. As the town progressed, music was provided by Silvey's Cornet Band led by M. J. Silvey. For many years during the summertime, Saturday night open-air concerts were enjoyed by all at Foxtail Park (now Sheridan Park) on North Tehama Street. Later John A. Apperson organized an orchestra and also composed a number of songs, including "Come and See Glenn County." Both of these musical groups brought much needed entertainment to not only the local townspeople but also to the entire county at fairs, dances, theatrical productions, and celebrations.

On January 16, 1890, the Willows Athletic Club was organized. There was great interest in baseball, with intense rivalry with neighboring towns. Other organizations that flourished were the Masons, Eastern Star, Odd Fellows, Daughters of Rebecca, Woodmen of the World, Native Daughters of the Golden West, and E Clampus Vitus.

Willows' first newspaper, the *Willows Journal*, made its debut on June 2, 1877. The *Willows Advocate* appeared for a short time, and on June 20, 1890, the first issue of the *Willows Review* was produced. The *Glenn Transcript* appeared on August 2, 1902.

Early-day doctors were W. C. Baylor, J. G. Calhoun, L. P. Tooley, Dr. Wilson, Francis X. Trembly, and Theodora Purkitt (first female doctor in Glenn County). Early dentists were Marian Pirkey, W. A. Sehorn, and R. F. West. The county hospital was built in 1898 at the north end of Colusa Street and was replaced in 1950 by the present hospital on West Sycamore and North Villa Streets.

The town was incorporated on January 4, 1886. City officials were A. A. Nordyke, G. W. Freeman, W. R. Merrill, W. C. Murdock, and W. C. Baylor as the board of trustees, with J. S. Gillum, clerk; P. H. Green, treasurer; and G. M. Potts, marshal. These good people had their work cut out for them with urgent need for fire and police protection, streets, and sewer, just to name a few of the items on a long list of needs.

In the early days of Willows, there were several disastrous fires driven by the north wind. The only firefighting method was a bucket brigade. With the organization of the Willows Water and Light Company in May 1887, adequate water pressure was established, and the town organized two hose companies with 60 members. The officers were Chief Henry Bielar; foreman of Glenn Hose Company No. One, J. F. Sersanous; and foreman of Willows Hose Company No. Two, J. D. Crane.

During the 1880s, there was much discontent among townspeople relative to the county government located in the city of Colusa, for Willows was a part of Colusa County at that time. They believed that their tax monies were mainly spent on the southern part of the county, while the northern end was generally ignored. A struggle to divide Colusa County into two counties ensued, led by newspapermen Frank Freeman and K. E. Kelley. A bill for the division of Colusa County was introduced to the California legislature on three different occasions, with success on the third try.

The new county was incorporated on May 11, 1891, with Willows as its county seat, for it was centrally located within the new county lines. It was named for Dr. Hugh J. Glenn, the "Wheat King," as $10,000 from his estate was donated by his heirs to the campaign for division, with the provision that the new county would be named for Dr. Glenn. The governor appointed a commission consisting of George H. Purkitt, chairman; J. N. Davis; M. B. Scribner; Joe Troxel; and Milton French to call an election to fill the county offices. County officials elected were Superior Court judge Seth Millington; sheriff P. H. Clark; clerk W. H. Sale; recorder H. B. Sanders; assessor L. R. Stewart; district attorney Ben F. Geis; treasurer James Millsaps; tax collector E. C. Kirkpatrick; auditor A. W. Sehorn; surveyor H. A. Hicks; coroner O. H. Martin; public administrator J. O. Johnson; and superintendent of schools William Finch. Supervisors elected were first district, H. C. Hulett; second district, J. F. Pieper; third district, N. B. Vanderford; fourth district, William M. Johnson; and fifth district, Philander Stone.

The courthouse cornerstone was laid with much fanfare on February 17, 1894, and this stately building is still in use today.

The *Colusa Sun* newspaperman Will S. Green must be credited with bringing irrigation from the Sacramento River to this arid valley. He devoted over 50 years of his life in designing, engineering, and promoting the Central Canal. Unfortunately he did not live to see water running through it. He died on July 2, 1905; however, others recognized the need for a local irrigation system, and over the years, it evolved into the Glenn-Colusa Irrigation District, which today provides the much needed water that transformed the valley into one of the most abundant agricultural areas in the world with rice, wheat, alfalfa, and row crops, to name a few.

In 1906, a group of civic-minded women organized a free reading room and library. They raised money and rented space in the Newman building on the corner of North Butte and West Walnut Streets. In 1910, a site for a new library on the corner of North Plumas and West Walnut Streets was purchased, and a Carnegie Grant for the new building was applied for and received. The beautiful structure served the community until 1969 when the library moved to the new civic center on North Lassen Street, but in 1972, it was transformed into The Museum and continues to serve.

On June 5, 1917, the eligible young men of the county registered for the draft for the war that was being fought half a world away. Willows went all out in the war effort, and Glenn County was the first county in the United States to subscribe its maximum quota for the Second Liberty Loan of 1917, a great portion of which was taken through the local banks. When the war ended, general pandemonium broke out, the *Willows Journal* published a 2:00 a.m. extra edition, the fire bell clanged, and a parade of many automobiles, with horns honking and flags waving, toured town. The Civic Memorial Hall, built in memory of the men who served in World War I, was dedicated on April 19, 1930, and is still a vital gathering place.

At one time, Willows had a large Chinese community. A number of them had been employed in the construction of the railroad tracks, and when that was completed, they found other pursuits such as cooks, laundrymen, and gardeners. Their settlement was located on the east side of the railroad tracks where the Western Concrete Ready-Mix Company presently is on Canton Street (named in memory of this settlement). It covered two blocks and several hundred people had their homes there as well as several stores, laundries, opium dens, and gambling places. When a fire completely destroyed this settlement in 1888, a new "Chinatown" was erected on Colusa Street between East Sycamore and East Willow Streets. Around 1900, Chinese families began to immigrate here, and the settlement continued until 1920 when most of the local Chinese population moved to San Francisco. Many had invested in rice lands and suffered financial losses in an extremely wet season that year when they could not harvest their rice crops.

On May 8, 1929, the Rialto Theatre opened its doors for the first time. It was located on the south side of West Sycamore Street, in the 200 block, and was constructed by the Griffith-Hunter Company, who had just finished building the Baptist church on the corner of North Lassen and West Walnut Streets. The Rialto was replaced in May 1950 with the Tower Theatre just one block to the west.

On June 1, 1929, the Willows Airport had its grand opening ceremony with an estimated crowd of 4,000 attending. That same year was also the beginning of the Willows Flying Service started by brothers Floyd and Dale Nolta. They purchased a World War I "Jenny" training airplane, which the innovative brothers fitted with a seed sower, and were the first in the state of California to seed rice from an airplane.

The 1930s arrived, and with the new decade, came the Great Depression, which was brought on by the stock market crash in the fall of 1929. The Bank of Willows, which was established in 1880, closed its doors in January 1933. It did, sometime later, reimburse its depositors 100 percent. The bank was liquidated and the building sold in early 1934 to the First National Bank of Willows.

Sheep-raising was a large industry, particularly in the surrounding area. According to the Glenn County Department of Agriculture, the sheep population in Glenn County in 1937 was 71,522, but in 2005, it was only 7,212. During the Depression, in 1933, a Willows butcher, Bill Weinrich, suggested to the local chamber of commerce a one-day celebration called a "Lamb Derby" to bring people to town and perhaps help the sagging local economy. Plans were made for a parade; a sheep show, including lamb races for the youngsters; and an evening grand ball. It was a huge success, and the celebration continues to this day—every Mother's Day weekend.

On October 16, 1940, two thousand young men of Glenn County registered for the draft, as there was a war raging in Europe once again. When Pearl Harbor was attacked, the United States entered the war, and as in the last world war, Willows joined in the war effort with victory gardens and the organization of a Ground Observers Corps to watch the skies for enemy aircraft. At the end of World War II in 1945, sixty-seven young men from Glenn County did not return.

In 1955, upon the suggestion of Joseph B. Ely with the Mendocino National Forest Service, Floyd and Vance Nolta developed a gate for a Boeing Stearman Caydet Agricultural Aircraft permitting it to drop their entire load of fire retardant at once upon a forest fire. The first airdrop on an actual wildfire in the Mendocino Forest was on August 13, 1955, flown by Vance Nolta. This aircraft became the first regular free-fall air tanker in the history of aviation. The device was adapted by the U.S. Forest Service, and it became a vital medium in fighting forest fires nationwide.

Willows had a very intense building program the first two decades of the 20th century but very little from the 1930s through the 1950s. Downtown had many empty dilapidated buildings, streets were deteriorating, the sewer system was inadequate, city hall was falling apart, and the library held far more books than the quantity for which it was built.

In 1966, several meetings were held where a number of objectives were formed, namely redevelopment of the downtown area, construction of a combined city hall and library, expand and upgrade the sewer system, provide for recreational needs, and encourage industrial development. The wheels began to turn, and in 1967, the sewer system was updated. After two failed bond issues, the city council used the lease-purchase plan to build a new civic center, which housed city offices, police, and library. A new fire station had already been constructed in 1962.

The urban renewal plan involved a two-block area in the downtown district from West Willow Street on the north to West Sycamore Street on the south and from North Tehama Street on the east to North Butte Street on the west. All of the buildings in this area were demolished, except for Daughtrey's Department Store (formerly Hochheimer's) on the southeast corner and an office building diagonally across from it. A $3 million shopping mall comprised of 100,000 square feet was built, and the First National Bank constructed new quarters in the area just south of the mall.

In 1975, Johns-Manville Fiberglass Insulation plant located here and began production in September. It employed approximately 150 workers.

Over the last 133 years, Willows has grown to be a city of 6,000 residents, but one thing remains constant, and that is its can-do and neighbor-helping-neighbor attitude. You can visit the big cities, mountains, and Pacific Ocean, all within easy driving distance, but it is always so nice to come home to Willows.

The Museum tells the story of Willows and its surrounding areas with photographs, artifacts, and many interesting displays sharing the history of our town. Elizabeth Eubank, city librarian for many years, cited this in her Glenn County Directory, 1947–1948, and we concur "To be ignorant of what happened before you were born is to be ever a child. For what is man's lifetime unless the memory of past events is woven with those of earlier times?"

One

OUR TOWN BEGINS

Just east of the present site of Willows, there was a great water hole shaded by willow trees. It was known near and far as "the Willows." This unique water hole is explained by an early historian, Justus Rogers, who said, "Several drainage creeks from the Coast Range joined here, and the land seemed to be capable of holding water, for there was a deep pond, something like half a mile long." It is said that this pond furnished water for as many as 5,000 cattle.

A Wintu Indian, Wallace Burrows, stands before the reconstructed roundhouse at Grindstone Indian Rancheria in this 1940s photograph. At one time it is said there were as many as 10,000 Wintu inhabiting the wide valley on the west side of the Sacramento River in Northern California, migrating according to the weather and food preferences. Most Wintu lived near the Coastal Range foothills to the west, where there was abundant water, wild game, ample fish in the streams, and plenty of edible plants, especially acorns, which were a staple food. Grasshoppers were a nutritious delicacy! The women were excellent basket makers. Winter homes were dugouts topped with a willow framework and covered with wet clay, so that Native American village looked like a cluster of low, smooth hills. An early traveler told of coming upon such a village and seeing children lying on top of each hill sunning themselves. As he approached, they all disappeared down the smoke holes of the dugouts. White man's diseases are blamed for the deaths of thousands of Wintu. Only a small number of native people remain in Glenn County, several of whom still prefer to live on the small Grindstone Rancheria north west of town.

Mary Ogle Zumwalt, 1804–1885, was
born in Pennsylvania. In 1849, she
came to California with her husband
and children in a covered wagon
drawn by oxen. She experienced the
deaths of six of her 14 children.

Joseph Zumwalt, 1801–1896, was born in
Kentucky. He married Mary Ogle on April
26, 1822. They were the parents of 14
children, one of whom was Daniel Zumwalt.
They were part of the influx of forty-niners
who came to California to seek their fortune.

Daniel Zumwalt, 1833–1927, was born in Indiana and came to California with his parents when he was 16. He eventually settled in what is now Glenn County and made a home for himself in what is now Willows. He married Nancy Murphy, had seven children, and lived to the age of 94. He is responsible for the original development of the town, having sold land to Charlie Crocker, owner of the Northern Railway Company.

DANIEL ZUMWALT
1833-1927

This train was photographed around 1900 at the Willows Depot with dignitaries posing and lined up next to the locomotive and railroad porters wearing their lightweight, protective dusters. The very first train into Willows had arrived on September 26, 1878, with much the same fanfare, including a brass band.

Willows railroad men and boys are pictured in 1886. Clarence R. Wickes is in the third row, center. This crew more than likely worked on the railroad out west of Willows toward Fruto. A similar but earlier crew would have worked for the Northern Railroad, laying track as well as developing roads through Willows, following the "high and dry" routes of earlier settlers.

Willows Train Depot is pictured in 1910, conveniently located across the street from accommodating hotels, saloons, and a livery stable. The buildings in the background are still standing, minus the awnings.

This view is along North Tehama Street before the tragic fire of 1920.

The IOOF (Independent Order of Odd Fellows) building was located prominently in the 200 block of Tehama Street. The date of its beginning, as shown on the building itself, was 1892. Note the combination of horses and early automobiles parked along the dusty street.

Milton French is said to have been a "self-made man." At the age of 12, he was orphaned and homeless, yet industrious and independent. In 1850, at the age of 17, he set out to make a living in the West. In 1858, he first settled 12 miles northwest of present-day Willows. He described the treeless plain, saying that between his place and Princeton "but one house, if a box set up on the plains could be so designated." French eventually took up a government claim of 160 acres in the western foothills of what is now Glenn County and gradually increased his holdings. He farmed thousands of acres of wheat, along with cattle, fine horses, and mules.

The Milton French home is located at 611 West Wood Street. French became active in the formation of Glenn County and took a leading role in many enterprises in which he invested large sums of money. In 1874, he married Elizabeth F. Williams, with whom he had three children: Curry, Rita, and Natalie. French was said to have been "just in his dealings and glad for the prosperity of others." When he passed away at his home on November 10, 1916, the whole county mourned his loss.

This early view toward Tehama Street from North Colusa Street shows the end of the railroad tracks at Willows. The west side of Tehama Street was populated, but the east side was railroad property and was not available for building. The Central Pacific Railroad eventually leased property on the Tehama frontage for business use but not residential. Warehouses were constructed on rail sidings visible on the left side of the photograph.

The Crawford Hotel was located at the southwest corner of North Tehama Street and West Sycamore Streets in the early 1900s. The hotel was owned by Col. Fred G. Crawford and was destroyed in the 1920 "Million Dollar Fire."

Hochheimer's second building, pictured in 1890, was located at the corner of West Sycamore and North Tehama Streets. It soon became a Willows landmark, housing many businesses over the years. Joe Troxel was taken in as a partner and later Amiel Hochheimer. Hochheimer's original partner, William Johnson, sold out in 1878.

Hochheimer's advertised, "Ten big departments under one roof."

Looking west toward Walnut Street, an early downtown business displays a "Furniture" sign. Well before 1900, a *Pacific Life Magazine* writer was quoted to say downtown Willows was "the most active business place of its size in California."

This millinery establishment is thought to have been in the 100 block of North Tehama Street near Walnut Street. It is undocumented, but the photograph is thought to have been taken around 1918 when Tom Ajax had a shop in a similar location, where he specialized in tailoring men's and women's clothing and selling lovely hats. One local historian remembers going there as a child with Jessie King and watching beautiful hats being brought out one by one for Jessie to try on. Tom the tailor was also manager of the Willows Giants, the first baseball team.

Timothy Reidy was born in Ireland in 1830 and came to California when he was 12. He worked as a blacksmith in several places, returning east and then traveling the world before coming to Willows in 1876. He continued the blacksmith's trade and soon owned the corner of North Butte and West Sycamore Streets, where he operated a busy shop, a meeting place where neighbors and friends often stopped to chat. Timothy married Kate Kinman in 1869 and they had three children: William J., Joseph M., and Sadie F. Reidy, who taught school for many years in Willows.

Farm hay was brought in from the field to the storage site to provide winter feed for livestock.

Mr. Seymour is shown to the left of his mule corral, and foreman LaRue is in the foreground. Mules were most often fed barley and hay. Some were also given grain night and morning. Stable hands cleaned the barns, fed the mules, and pumped the water. Working mule teams were watered as many as five times a day from tanks brought to the fields. In those early days before veterinarians, teamsters knew remedies for common mule afflictions and doctored their own animals.

This mule-drawn harvester was on the Fred Quint ranch, as shown in 1902. Mules were used because they were able to withstand the heat better than horses. There are 21 mules on this team. The last mule, shown with its head down, was called the "wheeler." It kept the other mules in line. The small boy on the right, almost out of view, is Earl Elvridge, grandson of Fred Quint.

This 1902 harvest scene with a steam harvester was on the Fred Quint ranch, 5 miles east of Willows. For fuel, a conveyor belt carried straw to a bin and the straw was burned, producing hot water for steam power. If more thrust was needed, logs were thrown into the fire. The harvester was shut down on windy days because of the great danger of fire, which could spread rapidly!

The harvest crew is pictured in 1909, working on the George W. Snowden ranch, 9 miles southwest of Willows.

Harvesting with a mule team is pictured on the George Snowden ranch. Mules were preferred over horses because of their greater stamina. Their feet were harder and did not get so sore. Some mules were never shod.

George Washington Snowden was born in Illinois in 1856, one of 11 children. He came to California in 1877 and began farming for himself, renting the 4,000-acre Logan ranch and planting wheat and barley. In 1896, he bought the Killebrew ranch of 960 acres, located 6.5 miles southwest of Willows, to which he later added 320 adjoining acres and rented another section nearby. With his brother James, he extended these operations, ultimately becoming the largest grain grower in the valley.

The home of George Washington Snowden was on the northwest corner of West Sycamore and North Plumas Streets. Snowden, like many other Willows residents, owned and operated a ranch outside of town. In 1889, he married Elizabeth Woolf, and they had two sons and a daughter named Lorene, who taught music and art at the Willows School. She married Carl Lohse of San Francisco. The Snowdens were active Republicans and members of local fraternal lodges.

A 10-mule team is pictured around 1900, pulling a "train" of wagons loaded with bagged grain, with Henry Michael riding on top. Loads like this were hauled to the Sacramento River, probably to Sidds Landing, where it would be transferred to a steamboat going to market.

Strawns' Custom Threshing machine is shown working a field in the Ord Bend area, prior to the introduction of mechanical tractors.

A. E. Pieper is shown on his tractor in 1913.

In 1918, rice was hauled by truck from the fields, rather than by mule team. As bags were filled with rice, sewers deftly stitched the bags closed with special, sharp needles. Men prided themselves on their speed at this part of the production line.

Farm hands are seen shocking new mown hay to allow it to dry before hauling to the winter feed lot. A photographer is evidently recording the scene on his camera as the mower operator poses to have his picture taken.

Sheep-raising was one of the most productive industries in Glenn County for many years. Sheep could thrive on the native grasses, which grew on arid soils with very little water. Glenn County Agricultural Department reports show a sheep population of 71,522 in 1937, declining to 7,212 in the year 2005 due to increased regulations and costs of feed.

Dr. Theodora Tiffee Purkitt was born to John R. and Rebecca Terrill (Poage) Tiffee in Petaluma, California, but reared in Glenn County, where she attended public schools. She married George H. Purkitt on April 28, 1873. After living several years on a ranch, they moved into town. Theodora entered the Cooper Medical College, San Francisco, and graduated in 1894 with a medical degree and highest honors. She was the first female doctor in Glenn County. In addition, Dr. Purkitt was the mother of six children: Herbert; Claude; Theodore, who married Minnie Hume; Edna, who married Jack Knight; Georgie, wife of Homer Henley of San Francisco; and Rebecca, wife of Charles Lambert Jr. of Willows.

The home on the southeast corner of West Sycamore and South Lassen Streets was built for Dr. Theodora Purkitt and later was the residence of her daughter and son-in-law, Rebecca and Charles Lambert. There was a carriage house to the east, next to the alley. An office building now occupies that location.

The Glenn County Hospital is pictured in 1916, located at the north end of Colusa Street. Finally the hospital was replaced in 1950 by Glenn General Hospital, located at the northeast corner of West Sycamore and North Villa Streets.

Dr. Etta Lund is shown in this early, rare, acknowledged poor-quality picture as a young graduate in medicine. She attended Coopers School of Medicine, the forerunner of Stanford University Medical School. She happened to be in San Francisco at the time of the 1906 earthquake, remaining there to assist as much as she could as a young physician and humanitarian. She came to Willows shortly thereafter to join her husband, Charles, who had set up a practice of medicine in Willows. The day Charles picked her up at the train depot the temperature recorded 114 degrees. She claimed at least it was a "dry heat." At first, she was laughed at when she tried to enlighten locals regarding disease carried by the abundant mosquitoes and flies.

This photograph of the Catholic church also shows the rectory to the east. Out of sight to the south of the church was the parish hall.

The Presbyterian church was located at the corner of North Sacramento and East Walnut Streets in 1911. After the church had been vacant for several years, the Christian church bought it for $250 and moved it to the South Plumas Street and West Oak Street site where it was joined onto their church building.

The First Baptist Church of Willows, shown in 1919, was at the corner of West Willow and North Plumas Streets. A rectory behind the church was moved west one block when the old church was dismantled 10 years later.

The "new" First Baptist Church of Willows was completed in 1929, on the corner of North Lassen and West Walnut Streets. A generous donation from Elizabeth French, wife of Milton French, made the new building possible.

Rita French, daughter of Milton and Elizabeth French, married Judge Moody. She followed her mother's example and contributed funds to the First Baptist Church in Willows, this time to create a very large stained-glass window of "The Good Shepherd" in the front of the church.

The Christian Church of Willows was organized as early as 1877. In 1889, under the leadership of Nanie Wilson Murdoch, a niece of Dr. Hugh J. Glenn, along with Rev. Charles Young, who married the widow of Forney Glenn, oldest child of Dr. Glenn, a church with a fine belfry was built on the east side of the 200 block of North Butte Street. It stood until 1920, when it was moved to the southeast corner of South Plumas and West Oak Streets. In 1926, the church purchased the long vacant Presbyterian church building for $250 and moved it to the Plumas-Oak site where it was added to the existing building. It was torn down in 1975, and a new sanctuary was erected in 1995. The bell from the original church was recently installed in a new belfry.

The Methodist church in Willows was sided with shingles. It was located on the southeast corner of North Shasta and West Willow Streets. The church faced Shasta Street, and a parsonage faced Willow Street. The old parsonage is still on that lot.

An early 1900s Methodist church photograph includes Reverend Movely on the left. On the right are A. H. Willard and the second man identified as Charles Kittinger, designer and superintendent of the Carnegie Library building project.

Going for a buggy ride was as much a delight as it was a necessary means of transportation. This photograph is from the Kittinger family collection.

At one time, this Willows Grammar School stood on the north side of the 500 block of West Sycamore Street, where the Veterans Memorial Building is presently located.

Willows Grammar School was located across from the Glenn County Courthouse.

Willows Grammar School teacher Sadie Reidy poses with eighth-grade students on the front steps of school in 1909. From left to right are (first row) Hans Fedde, Hal DeGaa, Joe Muller, W. A. "Bill" Weinrich, Ed West, and Thelma Wickes; (second row) Ed Schnurbusch, Elsworth Rawlins, Amiel Goetsch, unidentified, Vivian Sehorn, and unidentified; (third row) Amos Horner, Laura Stout, unidentified, Marie Rose, and Sadie Reidy, teacher.

Sadie Reidy models a wedding dress, which was a family heirloom. She was the daughter of Tim Reidy, local blacksmith and businessman. Sadie was a longtime, respected teacher at Willows Grammar School.

Sycamore School is remembered by many locals and was located near the intersection of West Sycamore and South Culver Streets. Constructed in 1922 at a cost of $200,000, the building served as an elementary school until 1975, when it was declared not earthquake proof. Much unanticipated effort was required to completely demolish the building. Lovely Sycamore Park is now in its place, complete with playground, skateboard center, tennis courts, horseshoe pits, and swimming pools.

All who attended Sycamore School are partial to this 1969 photograph taken of the playground at the rear of the building. Children still play on the location, now called Sycamore Park, at the corner of Sycamore and Culver Streets.

40

The first Willows High School, pictured in 1912, was located on the west side of North Lassen Street, between West Walnut and West Willow Streets, facing east.

Moving the old Willows High School from North Lassen Street was quite a process but not unusual in those days. Charles Roberts was the moving contractor.

Glenn County High School burned down in March 1942. The high school yearbook, the *Tattler*, sadly recorded the event in photographs.

The Glenn County High School girls' basketball team poses for their picture in 1912. Lorene Snowden Lohse is standing to the left in the first row.

Willows High School was known as Glenn County High School in 1915. The baseball team was on a popular postcard. Pictured are, from left to right, (first row) Edmund West, Roy King, Ira Woodworth, Leo Feeney, and Hal DeGaa; (second row) Aubrey Rawlins, Alton "Stick" Davis, Leo Weinrich, Orbell Apperson, coach Weber, Leo Woodworth, and Dean Walker. Written on the back of the card to K. Wakefield was, "Dear Cos. Am sending you this year's H. S. team. Our book the *Tattler* will soon be out and I will send you a copy. I am playing 1st this year. Do you recognize me? So long . . . yours truly, Roy King."

The Glenn County High School class of 1928 is pictured with their school, located on Lassen Street at the corner of Walnut Street. Frances and Alice King are in the picture.

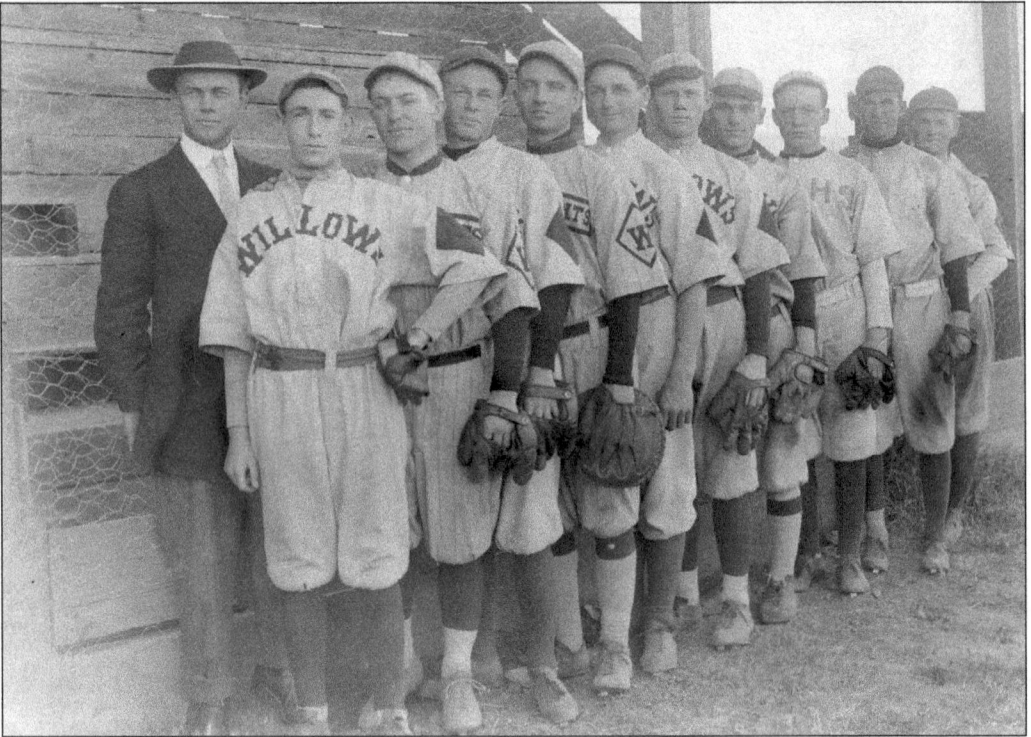

Mr. Yoder and his Willows baseball team are shown in 1917. From left to right are Hal DeGaa, Leon Marshall, Aubrey Rawlins, Edmond West, Dick Davis, Orville Apperson, unidentified, Ellsworth Rawlins, Leo Feeny, and unidentified. Many serious fans as well as players were devoted to the sport of baseball. In the late 1940s, the Willows Cardinals, a semiprofessional team, played at Ajax Field in Willows.

The Willows baseball team, pictured here in 1917, was called the Giants. They played on a field named for manager Tom Ajax. It was located opposite Birch Street, just east of the railroad tracks.

A popular form of fair-weather transportation for one or two people in the 1800s was this type of buggy. A horse-racing sport developed with one driver sitting in the buggy. A racetrack was built east of Willows. Everyone anticipated the weeklong series of races held in August. It is said that women prepared a different dress for each day. Crowds turned out. Trotter horses were shod by J. A. Reidy, a blacksmith like his father, Tim, who was a respected businessman in downtown Willows.

The horse track, where sulky buggies were pulled behind fast trotter horses, was east of the railroad tracks between Wood Street on the north and Glenn County Road 51 on the south.

John E. Knight was born on August 20, 1875. He married Edna L. Purkitt in July 1901, and they had three sons: John Richard Tiffee, George Purkitt, and Terrill.

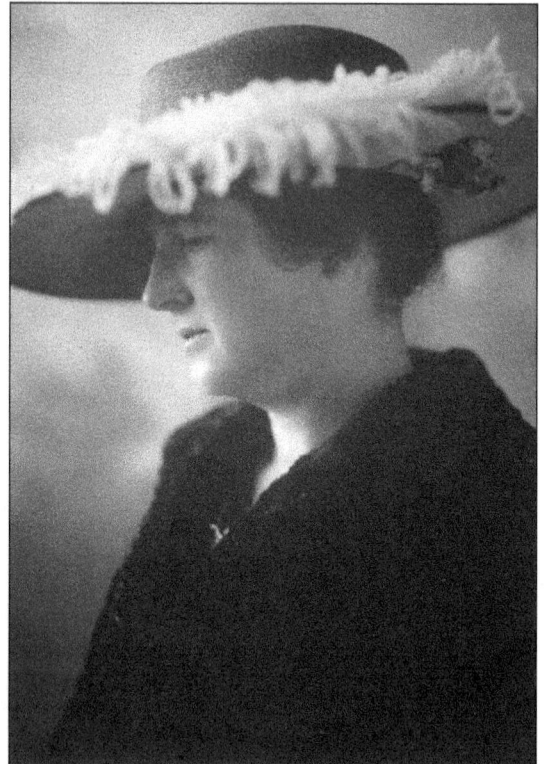

Edna Purkitt Knight was the daughter of Dr. Theodora Purkitt. This well-educated farm girl was the wife of John "Jack" Knight. She was well known for her prize Jersey cows, which she proudly showed many times in county fairs.

Jack Knight and Edna Purkitt went for a ride in a carriage while courting. They married in 1901. Is that a surrey with the fringe on top?

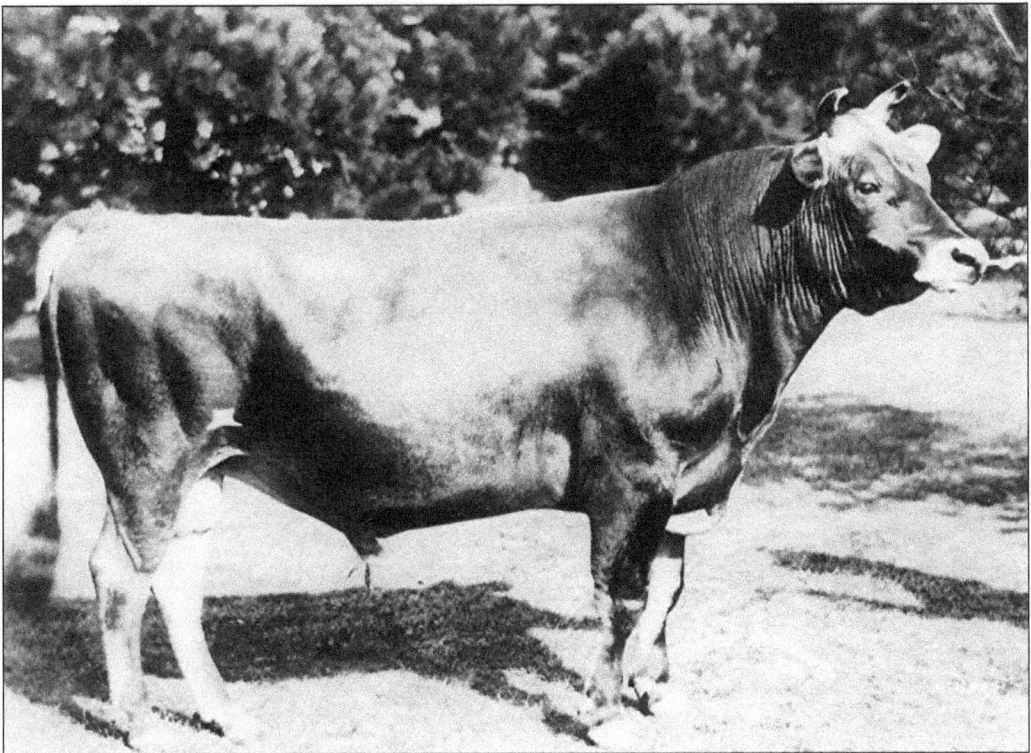

Blue-ribbon Jersey cattle were raised by Edna Purkitt Knight. She was owner/manager of the Willow-Meadow Jersey Farm Dairy and was active in civic affairs.

47

Young William Weinrich is in the driver seat, posing with his mother in their Overland automobile, which they proudly purchased new in 1912 for $1,760.

This early home was the residence of the Weinrich family, as pictured in 1912. It was located at 147 South Butte Street. The car out front was a 45 HP with a right-hand drive. Father Frank was at the wheel with Bill at his side. Mother Georgia, Frances, and George are pictured in the back seat.

Willows Meat Market was decorated for Christmas, as shown on this 1911 postcard. Pictured from left to right are William A. Weinrich, Frank B. Weinrich, A. Bair, Oscar Schnurbusch, Harry S., and Joe Gall. Note the decorative carvings on the fat of the hanging carcasses.

Buffalo hunter Frank Weinrich bagged this trophy in 1926. The head was mounted and still remains on the wall of the Willows Hardware Store in downtown Willows, keeping a watch on business.

Central Meat Market is freshly swept and ready for customers.

Looking at the south side of the 100 block of West Sycamore Street, this is a typical downtown scene in early Willows, with the Crawford Hotel on the left..

The Hochheimer Building is pictured on a summer day. Note the shady awnings on this busy intersection.

Sheridan Park is pictured in 1938. It is located on the east side of North Tehama Street, just north of Sycamore Street.

George Henry Purkitt was born in Illinois in 1838 to "good old colonial stock" on both sides of his family. A great-grandfather was a member of the Boston Tea Party and served throughout the Revolutionary War. George selected civil engineering as a profession, graduated from Jacksonville College, started for California with an ox team, and arrived in Sacramento on July 6, 1862. He followed hydraulic mining for a short time and then served as a Colusa County deputy sheriff in 1869. After marrying Theodora Tiffee in 1872, the couple moved to the northwest part of Colusa County and took charge of the Tiffee estate, a ranch located 9 miles west of Willows. There they lived and farmed until 1889 when they moved into town. Purkitt took an active role in politics, always a staunch Democrat. He was appointed by Governor Markham in 1891 to serve as chairman of a commission to call an election to fill the county offices for the newly formed County of Glenn. He was the father of six children: Herbert, Claude, Theodore, Edna, Georgie, and Rebecca. It was said that he was a man of unquestioned integrity and loyal to his friends in a marked degree.

The Glenn County Courthouse in Willows was constructed in 1894 following the incorporation of Glenn County, when Willows was named the county seat. The jail is seen to the right. The original building is still in use, minus its dome and statues, and the jail evolved into county offices.

The first Glenn County criminal trial jury in 1891 included (first row) Fred Hendrick, Henry Lohman, Charles Strawn, J. F. Vanlandingham, Al Merrill (foreman), S. G. Shirley, and George Yocum; (second row) George Hoffman, M. M. Boone, Tom Kincade, E. Squire, and Frank Davis.

Glenn County Garage was located on North Colusa Street in 1913. At one time, property at the corner of Enright and Laurel Streets was used as a Glenn County yard.

Naomi (Omi) Maddox and Dutch Rainville are pictured with both the old grammar school and the courthouse in the background.

The Klemmer home is pictured at 137 South Plumas Street. Note its proximity to the county courthouse.

The Scheeline home, covered in decorative shingles, was a gift to the newlyweds from their parents.

The home of Judge Seth Millington, around 1905, was located at 464 East Wood Street, at the corner of Fourth Street. He was the first Superior Court judge of Glenn County.

An early-day circus was coming to town! Is that a caged beast on parade?

A circus parade, around 1903, included costumed participants who delighted spectators in downtown Willows.

A circus is pictured on parade through Willows, with an interesting elephant!

Looks like a wild creature is being paraded through town in a circus parade! People came from miles around to view the festive event.

The Newman Building on the northeast corner of North Butte and West Walnut Streets was rented by the Women's Improvement Society to create a free reading room and library in 1906. Money was raised to pay the rent, purchase books and furnishings, and hire Ada Knock as librarian for $16 per month. The society members applied successfully for a $10,000 grant from the Carnegie Foundation to build a new free public library on the corner of Walnut and North Plumas Streets.

Charles Kittinger was the designer of the Carnegie Library building, which presently houses the Willows Museum. Kittinger took many photographs of the area, having spent portions of his childhood in Willows. The Kittinger collection is made available to the museum courtesy of Frank Prentice and includes Kittinger as a child at the local Methodist church Sunday school.

The Carnegie Library building is shown in 1910. The acknowledged poor-quality photograph is the only known view of the building under construction.

The classic-revival style library building was completed in 1911 with a $10,000 Andrew Carnegie Foundation grant. It was built by Graham and Jensen, having been designed by Charles Kittinger.

Louise Eubank, left, and her sister Elizabeth were both active in Willows civic affairs. Elizabeth served as librarian at the Willows Free Public Library beginning in 1918, until her retirement in 1962. She published a county directory in 1947–1948, which remains a vital source of information, not only for its telephone directory but also because of its wealth of historical information about Willows. Louise was city clerk for several years and served with the Red Cross in World War I, sending home mementos as she traveled.

Silvey's Band from Willows performed in front of the Bartlett Springs Hotel, date unknown. Silvey is in the center, facing the camera, with his cornet in hand. J. A. Apperson, well-known musician and composer, is fourth from the right.

H. D. DeGaa, longtime owner and writer for his *Glenn Transcript* newspaper is shown at his typewriter in 1921; Joe Muller is at left and Mattie Watkins is at right.

William Semple Green was born in Kentucky in 1932. He came to California at the age of 17, arriving finally in Colusa in 1850, where he was buried 55 years later. He held many and varied jobs, but perhaps the most effective and remembered was his writing career for the *Colusa Sun* newspaper, through which he proclaimed his vision and passion to bring water from the Sacramento River onto the vast northern Sacramento Valley in an elaborate irrigation system. Green lived barely long enough to see the system become reality. California has often been called the world's bread basket . . . a term which might not have been possible without Will Green's vision of water irrigating the land.

Two

BUILDING UP OUR TOWN

The Sacramento River is now controlled by the Shasta Dam north of Redding. In days prior to the dam, floods from the river happened regularly. The river provides much of the irrigation waters to the northern Sacramento Valley. More dams and canals are to the west, channeling water from the Coastal Range.

Sacramento Valley Irrigation Company pumping station was under construction on the Sacramento River north of Hamilton City around 1910. The pumps are now operated by the Glenn-Colusa Irrigation District, headquartered in Willows.

Steam-powered draglines were used to dig miles of canals throughout the arid valley when the irrigation plan was implemented.

The irrigation project pumping station was vital to the flourishing of the valley.

The sign reads "Land Sales Department, Sacramento Valley Irrigation Company, H. L. Hollister & Co., Agents." The building still stands on East Sycamore Street.

"Come and See Glenn County" is a song published in 1907. Its composer, John Apperson, was a pioneer newspaperman in the north valley and stepfather of Nellie L. King, mother of Jessie, Frances, and Alice King.

A parade float is at the intersection of Tehama and West Sycamore Streets. The Sacramento Valley Irrigation Company was getting the word out that Glenn County was the place to be for the best farming. Note the sign hung over the street next to Hochheimer's, which reads, "Glenn County—Why?—Irrigation!"

The Crawford Hotel, in 1916, was located at the southwest corner of West Sycamore and South Tehama Streets. Along with many other buildings, the Crawford was destroyed by the great fire of 1920, called the "Million Dollar Fire."

This parade is shown going down Sycamore Street, passing the Hochheimer Building, which is fully decorated in Fourth of July red, white, and blue.

The parade shown here was moving west on East Sycamore Street.

Willows loved its parades. Sheridan Park was a convenient gathering place after the parade, set up with food and entertainment.

Royalty in the 1910 Fourth of July parade are, from left to right, Blanche Staton, Queen Naomi (Omi) Maddox, Dorothy Keyes, unidentified, Lola Neel (Wolcott), Marguerite Davis (Thurman), Ruby Bair (Mainville), and an unidentified male driver. This float is on West Walnut Street nearing North Butte Street. Bank of Willows with its tall flag poles is in the left rear of the scene.

A passenger train is shown arriving in Willows around 1914.

This view is looking west from the Willows City water tower at North Colusa and East Willow Street, with West Wood Street at the right of center and a railroad warehouse in the foreground.

The Reidy Building is located in the 100 block of West Sycamore Street on the south side, just west of the alley. This building is still in use, having accommodated many businesses since its original construction in 1910. Early settler Tim Reidy was a well-established businessman and blacksmith.

The Barceloux Building, shown under construction in 1910, is still in use on the southeast corner of West Sycamore and South Butte Streets. It has housed many businesses over the years.

Advertisements for goods on sale at Pieper's store appeared routinely in the local paper. Amiel D. Pieper was born on May 12, 1870, in Hamburg, Germany, and arrived in Willows with this parents and brother on May 4, 1882. He attended local schools. Amiel entered the mercantile business in 1888 when he went to work at Eppinger and Company in Germantown (Artois, Glenn County). He ultimately owned his own department store in Willows at the corner of North Butte and West Walnut Streets, best known as Pieper's.

The Green Building was constructed in 1911 on the southwest corner of North Butte and West Walnut Streets. For many years, it was known as Pieper's, a general merchandise store owned by Amiel Pieper.

The Masonic building is pictured in 1938 on the west side of North Butte Street. Erected around 1910, the building housed the telephone company for many years.

Dr. Deacon was open for business upstairs in the Barceloux Building at the corner of South Butte and West Sycamore Streets.

The Masonic Temple is pictured in 1912. It is still standing, located on the west side of the 100 block of North Butte Street.

Glenn County Savings Bank opened in 1911 and became the Liberty Bank in 1920. It was purchased by Bank of Italy in 1927, which in 1930 became Bank of America.

The original opera house built in 1910, as shown, was located on the south side of the 200 block of West Sycamore Street on the west side of the alley. In 1929, the Rialto Movie Theatre occupied that site, followed by the Bank of America. A barbershop and the newspaper office were just to the west.

January 1, 1916, turned into a snowy day, which was an unusual occurrence. This photograph is looking toward Tehama Street by the railroad, with Sheridan Park to the left of center.

The eucalyptus grove, which still thrives 4 miles north of Willows, was planted in 1912 to provide lumber for furniture. The wood tended to crack as it dried, making it unsuitable for that purpose, and the enterprise was deemed a failure and abandoned. Eucalyptus wood has proven to be very good firewood and is widely used for that purpose. It is possible that some eucalyptus wood may have been used in steam trains in the early days, turning firewood into power.

Crossing the Sacramento River aboard a ferry was the only way to get to Willows from the east side of the valley until bridges were built over the river. The Ord Bend Ferry was a popular crossing, just north of the Glenn Ranch at Jacinto northeast of Willows. Youthful memories include jumping from the ferry midstream and swimming to the east shore where a beach can be seen in the photograph.

Waiting to board the Ord Bend Ferry to cross the Sacramento River around 1915 were R. C. Jessee, driver, and Nettie Jessee. Bob Corbett noted that his mother, Lela Corbett, is the one standing talking to her parents. Harold Corbett, his father, is shown standing talking to people in the third Model T.

This home, which has a carriage boarding step made of concrete and embossed "Murdoch," is thought to have belonged to Pastor Murdoch, once assigned to the Willows Christian Church.

Corbett's Radiator Shop, in the 100 block of North Colusa Street, was a place where one could obtain the latest information about what was going on in town, as well as get a car fixed.

John (Jack) Knight's farm equipment and supply business was in the 400 block of North Tehama Street. Signs advertise "CASE" tractors and farm implements, as well as turkeys and poultry. Jack's wife, Edna, raised prize Jersey cows.

The Bank of Willows was a locally owned bank, first organized in 1880 with operations in the Crawford Hotel. The first president was N. D. Rideout, and the first cashier was W. C. Murdock. The bank was then located on the northwest corner of North Tehama and West Walnut Streets, as seen in the photograph, until its financial failure in January 1933 during the Great Depression. The First National Bank bought the building in 1934.

L–K Garage was located at the northwest corner of West Willow and North Tehama Streets.

Carl Lohse's Buick Agency was located on North Tehama Street, with its "assigned seating" out in front.

Edmund Schnurbusch
is pictured on horseback
in the early 1920s.

The Pirkey home at the corner of West Wood Street and North Murdock Street was later occupied
by Dr. Pirkey's daughter Marian and son-in-law Carroll F. Byrd. The house is east across Murdock
Street from the Milton French house.

The federal building, better known as the post office, was built in 1917. In addition to the post office on the main floor, it also housed the Glenn County Farm Advisor and the U.S. Forest Service on the second floor, both of which have since moved to other quarters.

The new post office faced south on the 300 block of West Sycamore Street. Construction is shown in progress in 1917.

The post office building nears completion in 1917. This view is of the east side of the structure on North Shasta Street.

The federal building, located on the northeast corner of West Sycamore and North Shasta Streets, was erected in 1917 at a cost of $75,000. It still houses the Willows Post Office. Upstairs once were the offices of the Stony Reserve of the U.S. Forest Service, later renamed the Mendocino National Forest, which has since moved to North Humboldt Street, and the Glenn County Farm Advisor's Office, which has also moved.

William A. Weinrich was a veteran of World War I.

James Boyd Sr. and his family are pictured here. A native of Ireland, Boyd came to California in 1868 by way of the Panama Canal. He first worked in a livery stable in Colusa and then came to what is now Glenn County and worked on ranches and leased land on which he raised grain. He married Clara M. Williams in 1889, with whom he had two children. Boyd was prominent in financial affairs and served as a county supervisor. It was said that the couple "endeared themselves to their friends, were public spirited and willing at all times to assist others."

E Clampus Vitus members, usually called "Clampers," are shown on parade along Tehama Street on May 21, 1918. One of the organizers of the Willows chapter was Tom Ajax, local tailor and manager of the baseball team for a time. The Clampers lodge formed back in the gold rush days to have fun, perform good deeds, and help widows and orphans. Many chapters are still active, with historic preservation high on their list of accomplishments.

The Palm Baths Swimming Pool was located on the west side of the 400 block of South Tehama Street. It was replaced by the city pool on West Laurel Street around 1948.

On July 11, 1920, around 3:00 p.m., a fire was discovered in the delicatessen of Hochheimer's department store. Usually the north wind is the culprit, but this time southwest winds fanned the blaze, and it was soon out of control. The fire was subdued around midnight, but by that time, 35

The "Million Dollar Fire" in 1920 is viewed from the Sycamore and Tehama Streets intersection. The remains of the Crawford Hotel are on the left and Hochheimer's smoldering remains are on

Willows Million Dollar Fire, July, 11, 1920.

buildings had been burned. A conservative estimate of the loss to the business community was placed at over a million dollars.

Willows Million Dollar Fire July, 11, 1920.

the right of Sycamore Street. The business section was rebuilt with the "can-do" attitude prevalent in Willows. Other improvements were accomplished as well in the next few years.

Holly Culver, 1888–1969, was born in Willows, the son of Mr. and Mrs. John C. Culver. His grandfather was Jacob Zumwalt. Holly married Martha Welch of Colusa, and they lived in Willows. He was a farmer. *Willows Journal* writer Charles Gleeson dubbed Holly the "first flying farmer." In his articles "Agricultural Aviation," he gave graphic accounts of "blood and feathers" and the antics of young flyers on duck patrols, as the birds were ruining rice, clover, and alfalfa crops.

Waterfowl hunters are pictured before there was a limit on the number of birds one could shoot. Now the Sacramento Valley Wildlife Refuge south of town, on the old Spaulding Ranch, provides a haven for the birds and peace for the farmers.

Always a popular sport, duck and goose hunting was encouraged and the killing of great numbers of waterfowl was allowed, because they were inundating the crops, which surrounded the area. In fact, many farmers hired "goose herders" to shoot into the air, discouraging birds from landing and decimating crops.

Firemen are extinguishing a fire in the Sterling Lumberyard on North Tehama Street, on the north side of East Walnut.

Around 1885, Willows organized two hose companies with Henry Bielar as chief. Up until this time, all they had to fight fires with were bucket brigades. With the organization of the Willows Water and Light Company, adequate water pressure was assured. Pictured above are, from left to right, Dell Stout, Hank Bealer, and Chief Henry Bielar.

Willows City Hall housed the fire department downstairs. City offices were upstairs, including an office for Dr. Etta Lund for a while in the 1940s. The city jail was also downstairs for a time.

90

This scene from the mid-1920s is in front of the Ellis J. Levy department store in the 100 block of North Tehama Street. The Levy store was previously occupied by Hochheimer's department store.

The Hochheimer Building on Sycamore Street housed a Safeway store and other businesses in the 1940s. Notice the sign indicating "Robt. E. Boyd Jeweler," and the dark sign that says "Drugs" over Mitchell's Drug Store.

The Hotel Barton is shown in 1935. It had opened for business May 1, 1926, on the corner of North Butte and West Walnut Streets, featuring 100 rooms, some with baths, an attractive dining room, and a large, inviting lobby. Rates were $1.50 and up for a single bed without a bath, single with bath—$2.50, and double with bath—$3.50. The business later became the Willows Hotel. It was destroyed by a fire in April 1981.

The Veterans Memorial Building was completed in 1930 at the corner of West Sycamore and North Lassen Streets as a tribute to the veterans of World War I.

Ellis J. Levy occupied the new Hochheimer Building after the 1920 "Million Dollar Fire" destroyed the previous building at the corner of Sycamore and Tehama Streets.

The Willows Meat Market is seen as it was in 1925 with owners George and Bill Weinrich.

Bill Weinrich is considered the father of the Lamb Derby. When the community needed a morale boost in the 1933 depression, Bill conceived the idea of a festive weekend in May focusing on Glenn County's number one producing livestock animal, lamb! Races, dancing, music, fire department water fights, a bucket brigade, and a parade were all part of the festivity. The tradition continues to this day.

Allan Burgi and Claire Marie Weinrich Rumiano led the pet parade in the 1934 Lamb Derby.

In the 1939 parade, Boy Scouts marched east on West Sycamore Street beside the Hochheimer Building.

Lamb Derby Queen in 1936 was Doris Nivens Kaiser.

Glenn County High School Band marched in many Lamb Derby parades under the direction of L. A. "Mac" McArthur. Many students enjoyed the privilege of learning to play a band instrument and/or twirl a baton under the tutelage of "Mac," who was known to amuse and delight the kids by walking on his hands . . . often causing loose change to fall from his pockets!

Sycamore School marching band is seen marching by Klines, a popular ice cream parlor. In 1942, two little girls, not yet in kindergarten, obtained permission and a nickel apiece to push their doll buggies up the alley to Klines for a one-scoop ice cream cone. They circled back around the block and were home, safe and sound, in no time, very proud of themselves. Ah, the good old days!

Leslie A. "Mac" McArthur was band director at Willows High School and Sycamore Elementary School from 1925 until his retirement in 1956. Both schools had marching bands and very active music programs.

George Otterson Sr. is shown riding his pet Brahma bull. He rode around the neighborhood and in many Lamb Derby parades.

Sheriff Roy Heard rode his horse in the 1940 Lamb Derby parade. In the background at the corner of West Sycamore and North Plumas Streets is the former residence of the George W. Snowden family, and to the far right is the Pieper residence.

In 1939, Lamb Derby celebrations were in their height of popularity. Started by Bill Weinrich in 1933 as a means of encouraging spirits in the Depression, the tradition continues each May to this day. Here children chase after lambs in a wild sort of race!

LEFT TO RIGHT
JOHN STOCK - ARMOUR & CO. BUYER.
R. R. De LAP - OFFICE MGR. JOHN CLAY & COMPANY.
DR. EDWIN BUNNELL - WILLOWS CALIF.
CHAS. E. SHOTWELL - SHEEP SALESMAN. JOHN CLAY & COMPANY
ROY F. GUY - SWIFT & CO. BUYER.
BUSCH STUDIO.

Lambs are shown being auctioned off to various buyers in white shirts. From left to right are John Stock from Armour and Company, R. R. De Lap from John Clay and Company, Dr. Edwin Bunnell of Willows, Charles E. Shotwell also from John Clay and Company, and Roy F. Guy from Swift and Company. Average weight was 77 pounds. Sale price was $16.75 per hundredweight (cwt).

Museum volunteer Bob Chittenden had his first plane ride in this cabin biplane as a child, at the 1939 Willows Air Show.

A low-flying monoplane thrilled the audience at the 1939 Willows Air Show at the Willows Airport west of town.

Three

RECOLLECTIONS OF
OUR TOWN

Fields were seeded from aircraft as early as 1919, when Dale and Floyd Nolta rigged their airplane with a seed sower, the first in the state of California. Before long, many farmers had their own planes. Some of those planes were outfitted to fight forest fires after the idea was implemented in 1955.

Crops have been seeded from airplanes since the 1920s. It is said that no other aspect of mechanization is more important to Glenn County agriculture than aviation. Of the 32,000 acres of rice in Glenn County, 98 percent is sown by airplane. In the early days when seed was sown dry by broadcast wagons and horses, it was considered a good day's work to sow 40 or 50 acres. Using an airplane, an average of 500 acres a day could be sown. Barley, wheat, clover, alfalfa, sudan grass, and other crops common to this district are sown by plane. Many farmers have learned to be pilots themselves.

A plane's hopper is filled with seed on the ground, so it can go up again quickly and continue the job while the wind is still.

Lee Sherwood stands beside his Boeing N3N plane at the Willows Airport around 1962. There were three commercial operators in agricultural aviation: Nolta Flying Service, Sherwood Flying Service, and Varney Air Industries.

Floyd Nolta's Twin Beech is set up to fight fires in 1960. In 1955, a whole new way to help fight fire was initiated from the Willows airport. According to Joseph Ely, "I remarked to Floyd Nolta that he sure had a lot of experience dropping things out of airplanes, and did he think he could do the same thing on a forest fire."

Flooding is a common occurrence in the valley. Locals say one can expect high water about every seven years. Before Shasta Dam controlled the Sacramento River, the valley received many more floods during the rainy season than in recent times.

The usually gradual banks of the Sacramento River at Ord Bend crossing are shown covered by the floodwaters of 1940.

Southern Pacific Railroad's water tower, as seen in 1944 at the corner of Tehama and Sycamore Streets, provided water for steam locomotives prior to the advent of diesel electric locomotives. The Mobile Oil service station adjoining on the south side advertised on the water tower.

Kyle Corson's Motor Inn garage is pictured in 1951 after a blaze, which was fanned by the wind. It was located in the 200 block of North Butte Street.

Zoe Dell West Nutter, "Theme Girl" of the 1939 World's Fair at Treasure Island, brought her delightful brand of glamour to town. From the mid-1940s to the mid-1950s, she taught tap and ballet dancing to hundreds of girls. She had a particular style and ability to transmit a love of dance to her students. Zoe Dell remains a friend to Willows and the Willows Museum.

An aerial view of Willows shows the high school between Lassen, Merrill, Wood, and Sycamore Streets.

The newly constructed Willows Airport is shown in this aerial photograph looking east across Willows.

Willows Department Store occupied the original Hochheimer Building, as have other businesses over the years. The one most recently remembered was Daughtrey's Department Store, where it is said "a person could buy just about anything, and always be in style."

I. G. Zumwalt Company was in this building on North Butte Street. Daniel Zumwalt's home was behind it to the north.

Willows Livestock Market, located on Glenn County Road 48 north of town, held a sale every Wednesday.

The Palace Hotel on North Tehama Street, pictured here in 1965, served as the Greyhound bus stop for many years. It is thought that this same building was the location of the indoor festivities welcoming the first train into Willows in 1878; the north wind forced the master of ceremonies and speakers indoors.

The Greyhound bus depot at 125 East Sycamore Street is pictured in 1961. It became Jimmie's Taxie, as many will remember.

Willows's fire engines are parked "at the ready" at the fire station on South Butte Street in 1976.

Fire chief Harry Schnurbusch poses with fire trucks in front of Willows City Hall around 1947.

Ajax field was located on Canton Street, south of East Laurel Street, just east of the railroad tracks. According to Earl Edwards, "You could look directly down Birch Street from the top of the grandstands." The field and structures were constructed in the early 1900s strictly adhering to semiprofessional specifications. The left field foul line ran approximately west to east, but slightly north to south, as was done then, with the priority of keeping the sun out of the batter's eyes.

The Ajax baseball field bleachers burned on a windy day in early summer of 1961. The facility was located at the end of Canton Street, just east of the intersection of West Birch and South Tehama Streets. Ajax field was named for manager Tom Ajax, a tailor by trade. The field was home to the Willows Cardinals, a semiprofessional team, beginning in the late 1940s. Visiting teams often stayed at the hotel on the corner of Butte and Walnut Streets.

Berkland and Fox Motors staff posed for this picture with the shop mechanics. Doc Fox is on the lower right.

Willows City Pool in Sycamore Park, near West Laurel Street, opened around 1948 and is still in use.

U.S. Interstate-5 freeway was under construction in 1965.

The Wood Street overpass was under construction in 1965.

This scene is on Wood Street, west of Willows, looking eastward.

During construction of the U.S. Interstate-5 freeway on the west edge of Willows, this detour was at Wood Street and the new overpass.

This 1965 view is looking east from the U.S. Interstate-5 Wood Street overpass.

With the new freeway west of town, local businesses started to migrate towards the freeway along West Wood Street, California State Route 162. This left many buildings vacant in downtown Willows. This is a view of Wood Street looking east from the I-5 freeway overpass.

Interstate-5 freeway was opened to traffic flow about 1968.

The county jail is shown as it appeared in the late 1960s.

The new civic center, completed in 1968, presently houses the city hall, police department, and public library.

The Museum has occupied the old Carnegie Library building in Willows since 1972. The Museum Society of Willows has been the recipient of countless artifacts, which are on display. Included in the collections are the photographs in this book.

Looking from atop the Masonic hall, one can see a unique view of Willows in 1969 when the old business section was still intact.

The buildings pictured looking north on West Walnut Street in 1968 were torn down to make room for the new mall shortly after this picture was taken.

Two blocks of downtown buildings were demolished during various phases of the redevelopment project. This is the First National Bank. There used to be buildings on either side.

Willows City Hall was burned during the redevelopment project in the 1970s.

A controlled burn to remove Linebaugh's Drug Store, located at the southwest corner of West Walnut and North Tehama Streets, was part of the redevelopment project of 1972.

Spectators enjoyed the activities as many buildings were demolished in the 1970s to prepare a place for the new mall along North Butte Street.

Demolition of old buildings was a sight to see and often drew crowds. Here the felling of buildings across from the Masonic building is watched by unidentified, Russ Ward, Gene Walker, Nick Stewart, and Dick Bond.

This photograph, looking southwest from North Tehama and West Willow Streets, was taken after most of the buildings were removed from a section of downtown as part of the redevelopment project. It presents a clear view of Butte Street in 1972.

In 1973, the redevelopment project mall was under construction at the corner of North Tehama and West Willow Streets.

The last crossing on the Ord Bend Ferry was in 1972, following the completion of the modern bridge, seen in the background.

The 1976 dedication of a memorial clock honors five local young men who died in the Vietnam War: Paul D. Brummet Jr., Michael E. Flannery, Ollie R. Stapleton, Thomas C. Ward, and Ernest B. Hanks III.

The beautiful fountain was part of the new mall developed in 1972 on the east side of North Butte Street, just north of West Walnut Street. The Vietnam Veterans Memorial Clock is visible to the right of center in the background.

The Willows Hotel, formerly Hotel Barton, was first opened to the public in 1926. It accidentally burned in 1981.

The Willows Hotel holds memories for a local resident who, according to her recollection, spent the first few weeks of her married life at the hotel until suitable rentals were available. Their memorable honeymoon was spent among duck hunters who occupied the hotel, complete with hunting dogs roaming freely through the building and feathers wafting from the basement, where skinning and plucking were taking place! The new husband felt right at home, being the future game warden in the area.

Old Sycamore School did not meet the Field Act earthquake safety standards, so they had to take it down around 1976. It stubbornly resisted being set afire before final demolition took place. Those were sad, frustrating days for many people, young and old. The location is now a beautiful park.

The Willows High School "Honker" band is pictured in the 1970s.

Frances King and her twin sister, Alice, smile for the camera around 1917.

BIBLIOGRAPHY

Baker, Sima, and Florence Ewing. *The Glenn County Story, Days Past and Present.* Willows, CA: Glenn County Schools Office, 1968.

Colusi County Historical Society. *Wagon Wheels.* Two volumes yearly, 1955–present.

Davis, Cynthia F. *Where Water Is King: Glenn County Irrigation District.* Willows, CA: Glenn County Irrigation District, 1984.

Eubank, Elizabeth. *Glenn County Directory.* Willows, CA: Willows Public Library, 1947-48.

Green, Will Semple. *History of Colusa and Glenn Counties.* San Francisco, CA: Elliott and Moore Publishers, 1889. Reproduced by Sacramento Lithograph Company for Elizabeth Eubank, 1950.

Lambert R., and C. D. McComish. *History of Colusa and Glenn Counties.* Los Angeles, CA: Historic Record Company, 1918.

White, Thelma. *Glenn County Sketchbook.* Butte County, CA: National League of American Pen Women, Butte County Branch, 1995.

DISCOVER THOUSANDS OF LOCAL HISTORY BOOKS
FEATURING MILLIONS OF VINTAGE IMAGES

Arcadia Publishing, the leading local history publisher in the United States, is committed to making history accessible and meaningful through publishing books that celebrate and preserve the heritage of America's people and places.

Find more books like this at
www.arcadiapublishing.com

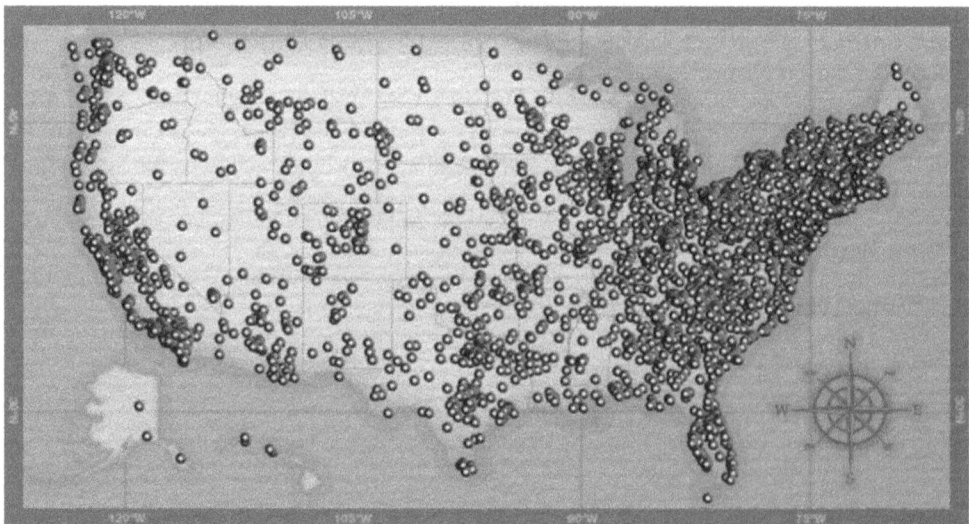

Search for your hometown history, your old stomping grounds, and even your favorite sports team.

www.ingramcontent.com/pod-product-compliance
Lightning Source LLC
Chambersburg PA
CBHW050613110426

42813CB00008B/2539